You

JoAn Stevenson

Illustrations by Kim Hanzo

TEACUP PRESS

www.teacup-press.com • www.foxpointepublishing.com/author-jo-an-stevenson

Library of Congress Cataloging-in-Publication Data
Stevenson, JoAn, author.
Farr, Chelsea, editor.
Hanzo, Kim, illustrator.
Hudson, Becca, designer.

You / JoAn Stevenson. – First edition.

Summary: An illustrated poem about a parent or guardian's love for their child.

ISBN 979-8-999883-75-9 (hardcover) / 978-1-952567-31-5 (softcover)
[1. Multigenerational Family Life – Fiction. 2. Emotions & Feelings – Fiction. 3. Poetry – Fiction.]

Library of Congress Control Number: 2 0 2 1 9 0 5 7 7 3

Second printing February 2026

For my dear grandchildren
who inspire me and color my world:
"The Littles," Emmett, Una, Gigi,
Greta, Odan, Emma, Cora,
and the older ones, Finlay, Elan,
Evan, Liam, Nicholas Jr., Avery,
Corban, and Tristan.

May you grow up surrounded
by love, joy, and happiness.
You are the ones I always dreamed of
and the children I will always love!

To their parents (my children),
Nicholas, Marie, Anthony, Lisa, and Sean,
with much love.

For every child who reads this book
because you are loved!

To my parents,
Robert & Lorene (Kruse) Simpson,
who taught me a love of reading at an early age.

To my Steven; thank you for your love
and support.

You are the *favorite story* I always tell.

You are the **wish** in the wishing well.

You

are the kite

flying high
in the sky.

You are the

huckleberry

in the pie.

You
are the
yellow
dandelion
chain.

You are the
rainbow
after the rain.

You
are the
lucky
penny
I found

and
the *book*
that
I
can't
put
down.

You

are the

firefly

dancing
in the
breeze

and
the
songbird
singing from
the trees.

You

are the

peanut

butter

and the *jelly*

and the

deep

laugh

that comes
from my belly.

You

are the *grass* tickling my feet

and my *favorite song* with the groovy beat.

You are the **candles** on the birthday cake.

You are the **morning mist** on the lake.

You

are the

paint

colorfully
swirled.

You are the

seven
wonders

of my world.

You
are the
lightning
and the
thunder
and the
umbrella
I take shelter under.

You

are the

owl

hooting in the night.

You are the

moonbeam

glowing so bright.

You are the **one** I always **dreamed of** and the child that **I will always love**

about the author

JoAn Stevenson is a fifth-generation Iowan and is now beginning a retirement career of writing books, mainly in the genres of children's and poetry. She has always been an avid reader and believes this is why she took up writing decades ago. Every year, she and her family members submit poems to the annual publication, "Lyrical Iowa."

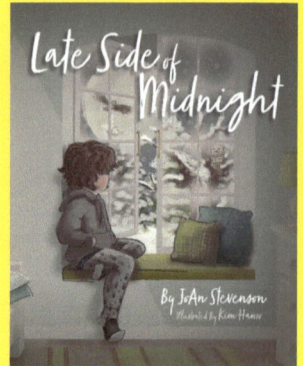

JoAn has five children and several grandchildren. She lives with three cats and enjoys reading, knitting, traveling, cooking, gardening, biking, and volunteering. Her favorite color is blue and she adores apple pie, Italian food, and potatoes in any form!

about the illustrator

Kim Hanzo is a graphic designer and illustrator who specializes in animal-inspired stories and imagery. She graduated from the Rochester Institute of Technology with a BFA in Illustration and an MFA in Painting. She has been a graphic designer for more than twenty years and founded her own greeting cards and prints company, Lellow Lolly, in 2016. Her work is available online and in several Hallmark stores in the US Southeast. Kim joined Fox Pointe Publishing in 2020 as a children's book illustrator. She also writes and illustrates her own children's books, including the "World of Difference" series starring animals with meaningful messages. She lives in North Carolina with her husband, three kids, mother, two dogs, four fish, and one guinea pig.

www.ingramcontent.com/pod-product-compliance
Lightning Source LLC
Chambersburg PA
CBHW041547260326
41914CB00016B/1578